MIGHTY MEN OF VALOR: BOOK 3

Passion

PRIORITIES FOR KINGDOM LIVING

MIGHTY MEN OF VALOR: BOOK 3

Passion

PRIORITIES FOR KINGDOM LIVING

Dean Ridings | Bob Jones | Scott Ballenger

Make a Mark
MINISTRIES

6660 Delmonico Drive, Suite D-140 · Colorado Springs, Colorado 80919

E-mail info@makeamark.net · Web www.makeamark.net
www.facebook.com/makeamarkministries

Mighty Men of Valor: Book 3

Passion

PRIORITIES FOR KINGDOM LIVING

Mighty Man of Valor's Name

Name and Contact Information of Warrior Brother(s)

Date Started

Date Completed

Iron sharpens iron,
and one man sharpens another.
Proverbs 27:17

Mighty Men of Valor: Book 3 – Passion

A Make a Mark Ministries Bible Study
Copyright © 2013, 2021 by Dean Ridings, Bob Jones, Scott Ballenger

This is the third in the series of Priorities for Kingdom Living, which includes:

Mighty Men of Valor: Book 1 – Strength
Mighty Men of Valor: Book 2 – Courage

Design: Steve Learned

Cover Photo: ©iStockphoto.com/GaryAlvis

Contents

Introduction

"Do not be slothful in zeal, be fervent in spirit, serve the Lord" (Romans 12:11). As the apostle Paul urged the church at Rome to be passionate in serving Jesus, so we welcome you to join us in growing more and more zealous about our great Savior.

Why passion? Because, from eternity past, the God of the universe chose each one of us and adopted us as His children. The Lord Jesus Christ loved us so much that He died in our place, taking on Himself all the penalty for sin that we deserve, and paying all the debt that we owe to God, setting us free from sin and giving us new life in Him. Mighty Men of Valor are passionate about their Lord and Savior.

So, do we run around with big Bibles so we can pound people over the head while shouting "Hallelujah"? No, God has a different view of passion and zeal in mind. Ours is a measured, controlled passion based on the truth of God's Word and expressed through a gentleness of spirit.

Jesus said it this way, "Blessed are the meek, for they shall inherit the earth" (Matthew 5:5). Think of Moses—confronting Pharaoh, calling on God to reveal His glory, leading perhaps two million people for four decades. Certainly here was a man passionate for God. Yet, God judged Moses as being "very meek, more than all people who were on the face of the earth" (Numbers 12:3).

The Mighty Men of Valor we see in Scripture and walking among us today have three distinct characteristics: They are men of *strength, courage, and passion.* As we did with strength and courage in the first two books of this series, here we unpack passion.

Men of valor love God above all else and live to serve Him with all the strength He has given us. It is our prayer that the lessons in this study will help you all the more serve as a man among Mighty Men of Valor who passionately live for good and for God in this generation—building others who will passionately live for Jesus in the next!

Using this Study

As with the previous Bible studies in this series, *Mighty Men of Valor: Book 3 – Passion* can be used in three essential ways.

First, you can use it as a daily devotional. We strongly encourage every man to take time out for a daily meeting—or *appointment*—with God. Make it a time of talking to God, looking into His Word, and asking Him to help you apply it to your life today.

Notice how Jesus, our example for life and ministry, made this a priority in His life. "And rising very early in the morning, while it was still dark, he departed and went out to a desolate place, and there he prayed" (Mark 1:35).

A second way you can use this study is to connect with other men—in the spirit of Hebrews 10:24-25—to stir up one another toward becoming Mighty Men of Valor. You may think of this as walking "Side-by-Side," meeting weekly for mutual growth, mutual support, and mutual accountability.

More than merely going through the Bible study together, it's all about helping one another "contend for the faith that was once for all delivered to the saints" (see Jude 3) in the midst of 21st century reality.

"Warrior Brothers" may be traditional mentoring or discipleship relationships between "mature" and their protégé "young" disciples, such as Elijah and Elisha or Paul and Timothy. Or they may be mutual discipleship or peer co-mentoring relationships between any two believers—no matter where they are in their faith—such as David and Jonathan or Paul and Barnabas. Proverbs 27:17 puts it this way: "Iron sharpens iron, and one man sharpens another."

Finally, a third way to use this study is in a triad or small-group setting. Think of Jesus, once again. He focused on a small group of men (see Luke 6:13-16). He built into their lives, strategically moving them along the discipleship journey. Yes, at times He fed thousands with physical and spiritual food; mainly, though, He invested in the Twelve.

If you're a man looking to make a key investment in other men, consider starting a small group. You might pray to have such an influence on a dozen lives. If you meet or exceed that goal, consider asking God ultimately to use you to invest in the lives of 300 men—like the small band that formed Gideon's army!

However you use this tool, remember that you are not alone. Along the way Jesus will both *guide* and *grow* you toward greater godliness (see Romans 8:28-29; Philippians 1:6; 2 Corinthians 3:18). Indeed, the Lord is with you, Mighty Man of Valor!

Bravery
Fighting the Good Fight

"Courage is not limited to the battlefield or the Indianapolis 500 or bravely catching a thief in your house. The real tests of courage are much quieter. They are the inner tests, like remaining faithful when nobody's looking, like enduring pain when the room is empty, like standing alone when you're misunderstood."
—Charles Swindoll

Read & Reflect

Read and reflect on Daniel 6:12-24. Consider the following question: *Why would a man stand steadfast with no fear in the face of sure death?*

_____

_____

_____

_____

The Challenge

As a young man, Daniel was taken captive from his beloved homeland of Judah to serve Nebuchadnezzar, king of Babylon. Daniel and his three friends were chosen to be trained as wise men in the court of the king. Yet even among his captors, this youthful man of God determined not to compromise God's Word. In every instance where Daniel might have had to stray from what God desired, he steadfastly held to the Law of God. And God exalted Daniel to be the chief adviser to the king. When the Medes conquered Babylon, Daniel became the favorite of king Darius as well.

A group of the other counselors, jealous of Daniel's favor, plotted together to get rid of him. Unable to find any fault in him, they tricked the king into signing a law prohibiting prayer to any god except the king himself. Anyone who broke this law would be thrown into a den of hungry lions. What would Daniel do?

Did Daniel compromise? Did he rationalize that the law was only in effect for thirty days so God would understand if he didn't pray? Did he reason that he was in such a position of influence it would be wrong to jeopardize his role with the king? Did Daniel try to sneak a prayer in when no one was looking? No! As soon as he heard the law, he immediately went to his home, got down on his knees in front of an open window and prayed for the whole world to see.

You see, Daniel had developed a habit of uncompromising obedience to God. Daniel had been faithful in little things and had seen God deliver him. Daniel knew that honoring God was even more important than saving his own life! He knew that God was not obligated to save him from the lions, but no matter; God must be exalted above all else. And what did God do? He delivered Daniel from the lions and had the beasts fed with Daniel's enemies. He can do the same for us.

Living It Out

His dad was a prominent Baptist pastor in Atlanta, and Martin Luther King, Jr., followed in his father's footsteps. While he preached God's Word, he found a national platform speaking out on civil rights issues in the midst of the turbulent 1960s.

It took bravery for MLK to seek to end racial segregation in the city's public transportation with his successful Montgomery bus boycott. It took courage for him to promote civil rights in partnership with other black Baptist ministers in the formation of the Southern Christian Leadership Conference. It took courage for him to tell the world about the dream God gave him of equality for all—no matter their ethnic or economic background—in his "I Have a Dream" speech delivered in Washington, D.C.

MLK's biblical conviction to "love your enemies" led to nonviolent rallies for a just cause, and ultimately to his violent death from an assassin's bullet. Yet what he so courageously stood for is making great strides yet today. Every January we remember MLK's birthday to honor this courageous man and the principles for which he stood.

———◆◆◆◆———

→ What is the risk when we choose compromise over courage?

_____

_____

_____

_____

→ How has your courage been tested? How did you do on the test?

_____

_____

_____

_____

→ In what area(s) of your life is God calling you to be courageous today?

_____

_____

_____

_____

Takeaway Truth

God's promises are reliable. God is holy, just, all-powerful, and He created you, all that you see, and all that you will become. He can be trusted with your concerns, and relied upon in times of need. This healthy dependence will give you courage when you need it. Now go and live today knowing that you will be tested, but you have what it takes to stand firm in God's Truth!

Valor Prayer

MIGHTY LORD, give me a strong conviction of Your truth, and the courage to stand firmly for it. With grace and love, I want to have the holy boldness of Daniel and Martin Luther King Jr. Help me to put the honor of Your name above my own fears. Be glorified in me, Lord! Thank You for working Your strength on my behalf.

For Further Investigation

→ Joshua 1
→ Acts 4:1-22
→ 1 Corinthians 16:13

Integrity
Keeping the Faith

*"I have more trouble with D. L. Moody
than with any other man I ever met."*
—D. L. Moody

Read & Reflect

Read and reflect on 2 Samuel 24:18-25. Consider the following question: *Why would a man choose "right" over "quick and easy"?*

_____

_____

_____

_____

The Challenge

King David was in a hurry. Because of his sin of pride, the nation of Israel was suffering the judgment of God; his people were dying, and it was his fault! God, speaking through the prophet Gad, told David that to stop the plague, he needed to raise an altar on the threshing floor of Araunah, a Jebusite farmer. Moved by grief and compassion for his people, David rushed to the farm, where Araunah offered to give him the land and the sacrificial oxen for free. Wow! What a deal! Not only could David save his people, he could also save time and quite a few shekels to boot. Who could refuse?

But David *did* refuse. He knew the full price of the site, and counted out the money for Araunah *before* building the altar and offering the sacrifice. Why would David turn down a gift and take more time to do so, especially in view of the circumstances?

The answer lies in David's integrity. David refused to compromise on what he knew to be right. He understood that taking such a gift would not be fair to Araunah. David the king would not take advantage of one of his subjects. Even more importantly, he realized that, while God's grace and forgiveness are free, the proper worship of God is never to be cheap or careless.

When a man comes before God, he must offer himself without reservation, no matter the cost. In his words, "I will not offer burnt offerings to the Lord my God that cost me nothing." For David's offering, God halted the plague and spared the people of Israel. He will do the same for us.

Living It Out

In 1505, a young Martin Luther was suddenly knocked to the ground by a bolt of lightning. "St. Anne help me!" he cried as he struggled to stand. "I will become a monk." This from the man who would one day spearhead the Protestant Reformation in response to injustices he observed in the Catholic church of his day.

"The man who thus called upon a saint was later to repudiate the cult of the saints," says the opening of his biography *Here I Stand*. "He who vowed to become a monk was later to renounce monasticism. A loyal son of the Catholic Church, he was later to shatter the structure of medieval Catholicism. A devoted servant of the pope, he was later to identify the popes with Antichrist."

How could he look the other way as his church sold "indulgences," being paid to forgive sins without repentance? For Martin, taking a stand against such practices was a matter of integrity. It was on October 31, 1517, that the young university scholar posted 95 Theses on the front doors of the Castle Church in Wittenberg, Germany. In so doing, he invited "scholars to dispute and dignitaries to define." Others, not Martin, spread his theses among the people. That's how his integrity ignited the Protestant Reformation.

───◆◆◆◆◆───

→ When have you chosen expedience rather than doing what you knew to be right? What was the result?

_____

_____

_____

_____

→ Why is it important to take a stand for the truth, especially when it comes to ministry within the church?

_____

_____

_____

_____

→ Is there a situation in which you need to bring truth to light? What's your plan?

_____

_____

_____

_____

Takeaway Truth

God's integrity is uncompromising. God does not take short-cuts with us, just look at His plan for redeeming mankind. God systematically revealed His plan through the line of Abraham and David. After 42 generations, He stepped out of heaven and became man to dwell among us in Jesus Christ! God is still in the process of redeeming mankind, and we are in the middle of His unfolding story. He is fulfilling His promise to us. Now go and live today as a godly man, relying on the integrity of God's plan to guide you!

Valor Prayer

HOLY FATHER, I confess that sometimes I am a hypocrite. Help me to walk the walk as I talk the talk. Help me to grow more and more like Jesus. Thank You for forgiving me. Thank You for giving the Holy Spirit to me. I pray that I will walk in the Spirit, and so glorify You.

For Further Investigation

→ John 1:47
→ Psalm 15
→ Psalm 78:70-72

Contentment
Satisfied Before God

"You say, 'If I had a little more, I should be very satisfied.'
You make a mistake. If you are not content with what you have,
you would not be satisfied if it were doubled."
—Charles Haddon Spurgeon

Read & Reflect

Read and reflect on Acts 16:22-31. Consider the following question: *What should be the response of a godly man who is unjustly treated?*

_____

_____

_____

_____

The Challenge

The apostle Paul suffered much torture and pain at the hands of the very people he loved and sought to help. Called by God to be the apostle to the Gentiles, Paul encountered opposition wherever he went. On this occasion, he and his friend Silas came to Philippi bringing the good news of forgiveness in Jesus Christ. Greedy businessmen, angry that Paul had compassionately healed a young woman of demonic possession, falsely accused Paul and Silas of treason against Rome.

So instead of being welcomed to the city, the two men were beaten, thrown into prison, and clamped into stocks to await the pleasure of the city magistrates. Surely this is not what the great apostle expected when God commissioned him to preach the Gospel! How easy it would be to become bitter at this undeserved suffering! Yet that is not what we observe.

After enduring the beatings, still bound in the stocks, we find Paul and Silas singing hymns and praising God. And not only singing and praising, but when the opportunity to escape opens up, the two men stay right where they are. Why? They had internalized the magnificent truth that life is not haphazard but that God is in control. They were content with any and every circumstance because they knew that they were in the hands of the Creator of the universe who promised to be with them always. God had allowed them to be thrown into prison, so God was going to honor Himself through their suffering. And how did God use their experience? Their jailor and his whole family came to Christ through the witness of Paul and Silas. And God can do the same with us. If you asked Paul if he thought his suffering was worth it, what do you think he would say?

Living It Out

John Bunyan was born near Bedford, England, in 1628. His love for the Bible helped him make sense of great loss early in his life with the deaths of his mother and sister. He was drafted into the military at 16, serving three years. One particular event marked him for life: the death of a young man who went on a mission in John's place. God had spared his life, he believed, for a special purpose.

Yet John would endure much despair in his days. His first son was born blind; after the births of three more children his wife died. He went through a dark spiritual season, questioning his faith. He emerged refined, cleansed, content to serve the Lord preaching. But when England ended the freedom of Non-conformists, he wouldn't stop preaching and was imprisoned for 12 years.

It's said that that's when he began to write the story of a man named Christian who went on an adventurous journey from the City of Destruction to the Celestial City, whose builder and maker is God. The book, *Pilgrim's Progress*, is not merely a literary masterpiece; it illustrates every spiritual man's journey and reflects that being a content Christian this side of heaven is no fairy tale.

———◆•■•◆———

→ Perhaps Paul didn't expect such suffering when God commissioned him to preach the Gospel. What did you have in mind when God called you into His Kingdom?

_____

_____

_____

_____

→ When have you felt bitter about the way you've been treated even as a Christian?

_____

_____

_____

_____

→ How does it help you to know that life is not haphazard but that God is in control?

_____

_____

_____

_____

_____

Takeaway Truth

God is enough. God is the Creator, Sustainer, and Provider of all. He is sufficient for all of our needs, hopes, dreams, and desires. When we depend on God for all of our needs, we glorify Him with our dependence upon Him. In fact, the more we get to know Him, the more we realize that it's *desperate dependence* upon Him! Now go and live today in thanksgiving and praise to the giver of true life!

Valor Prayer

LORD JESUS, life is often hard, especially when I feel like I have to face it alone. Thank You that You promised to be with me always. You said that Your yoke is easy and Your burden is light. Help me to be content in every circumstance of life because my life is in Your all-powerful hands.

For Further Investigation

✦ Proverbs 30:7-9
✦ Philippians 4:11-13
✦ Hebrews 13:5

Generosity
Openhanded in Everything

*"You may think, 'No problem there. I'm putting my church and
ministries in my will.' By all means, do your estate planning and
give heavily to God's Kingdom. But what kind of faith
does it take to part with your money once you die?
You don't have any choice! Death isn't your best opportunity to give;
it's the end of your opportunity to give. God rewards acts
of faith done while we're still living."*
—Randy Alcorn

Read & Reflect

Read and reflect on Acts 4:32-37. Consider the following question: *Can you imagine a church where there is no person in need
because God's family is coming through?*

The Challenge

Like any big city today, Jerusalem in the time of Christ was
a mixture of wealthy, middle class, and poor. As the Gospel
spread throughout the city, the church became a miniature
reflection of the people there. There were new Christians who
owned much land and houses, as well as those who struggled
to make it through each day. How would the church respond?
What kind of witness would this young faith be to the watching

city around them? Did Jesus Christ really make a difference in their lives, or was this just another sect of Judaism founded by a charismatic leader?

Here in this passage is a community of people who were radically filled with the love of Christ. Every one of them single-mindedly committed to Christ and to one another. The big businessmen gladly sold their beach houses and blue chip stocks and gave the money to the poor. If someone had two coats, he gave one to a person who had none. If one among them was hungry, another sold his mountain property and provided groceries. They were family, and they willingly sacrificed for one another. The more they experienced the grace of God, the more generous they became.

As a result, *there was not a needy person among them!* And God continually brought more and more people to Christ through the witness of His family. More than we may realize, God is doing the same today. Are you getting in on all the giving?

Living It Out

George Müeller was born and raised in Prussia during the 1800s, yet he faced struggles common to man. Even as he studied for the ministry he dabbled in "sin and crime." That all changed when he asked Jesus into his heart during a prayer meeting.

He tried unsuccessfully to become a missionary in the Orient, so he started to preach the Gospel wherever he could. In 1834 he began the Scriptural Knowledge Institution to send missionaries, Bibles, and Gospel materials around the world. The following year he opened an orphans' home for 26 girls.

All told, the Institution trained more than 121,000 students and distributed some 300,000 Bibles, 1.5 million New Testaments, and 111 million tracts. Meanwhile, he built five orphans' homes, which fed 2,100 orphans every day.

When it came to finances, remarkably, George shared his

needs only with God in prayer. And like manna from heaven, the money came in. It's estimated he received $7.5 million, all of which he used to spread the Gospel and care for orphans. Even the personal gifts he received through 70 years of ministry—valued at some $500,000—he donated to the Institution. When he died at 93, his estate was valued less than $1,000, for he had given away the rest for the cause of Christ.

→ On a scale of 1 ("not a giver") to 10 ("sold on giving"), where are you? Why?

_____

_____

_____

_____

→ Where have you seen your giving efforts multiplied by God? As a donor, how has that affected you personally?

_____

_____

_____

_____

→ How have you benefited from God's provision through His people? Take a moment to thank Him for all that He has done and is doing!

_____

_____

_____

_____

Takeaway Truth

Everything belongs to God. Everything that we have: our time, talents, treasures, and family . . . they're all entrusted to us from God during our time here on earth. The question is, what will you do with all you've been given? Now go and live today with an open heart and open hands sharing what you have been entrusted with!

Valor Prayer

SOVEREIGN GOD, Your Word tells us that the earth is Yours and all it contains. I release my money, my possessions and all that I have into Your hands, because You own it anyway. Help me to see the needs of my brothers and sisters in Christ. Help me to generously give, not only to meet their needs, but to build Your kingdom around the world. Give me wisdom to see where my giving can be most effective for Your glory. Thank You for meeting my every need.

For Further Investigation

→ 1 Chronicles 29:14
→ Matthew 6:1-4, 15-23
→ Galatians 6:7-10

Service
Here to Serve

"The only really happy people are those who
have learned how to serve."
—Albert Schweitzer

Read & Reflect

Read and reflect on Acts 6:1-7. Consider the following question:
What happens in a church when men serve?

_____

_____

_____

_____

The Challenge

The apostles were gifted men, called by God to lead the new Christian church, but they were not supermen. As the young church grew in number, all sorts of difficulties arose, and for a while the apostles took care of each problem personally. But the administration of the church finally reached a crisis point when Greek-speaking Jews complained that their widows were being short-changed in the distribution of food.

That's when the apostles realized they were neglecting God's call to preach and teach in order to take care of the daily routines of the assembly. So what did they do? They called for a band of brothers. They asked the church to choose "seven men of good repute, full of the Spirit and of wisdom" (Acts 6:3).

The church was happy to do so. They picked seven of their

number and set them up as a team to take care of daily business in the church, with the blessing of the apostles. Here were men who loved the Lord and took the risk of serving His people. Their ministry not only helped ensure fair treatment to the entire congregation, but it also freed up the apostles to carry out the mandate given to them by Jesus. These men were vital to the beginning of the Christian church. "And the word of God continued to increase, and the number of disciples multiplied greatly in Jerusalem" (Acts 6:7a). Today, God still grows His church through men who are willing to serve.

Living It Out

Jimmy Carter was the thirty-ninth president of the United States. After his 1981 White House departure, however, he earned praise across political parties for his efforts to serve people in need around the world. He considered it a natural demonstration of his Christian commitment. Among other activities, the nonprofit Carter Center he and his wife founded works to improve health around the world. For its humanitarian work he received a Nobel Peace Prize.

In his latter years, he was surprised that the most well-known aspect of his public service was reaching out to needy families through Habitat for Humanity, an organization dedicated to building homes for the world's down and out. For several decades he devoted himself to working side by side with poor families to build their own houses across the United States and in a number of foreign countries.

Why serve? In *Our Endangered Values* (Simon & Schuster, 2005), he wrote: "This has been an enjoyable and heartwarming opportunity for us and many others to put our religious faith into practice, and it demonstrates vividly the importance and difficulty of reaching out to needy people."

→ Jesus said He didn't come to be served but to serve. To what extent does that reflect your mission as well?

_____

_____

_____

→ It's often said that those who serve benefit more than those being served. Has this been your experience?

_____

_____

_____

→ What steps might you take today to make serving others more of a daily priority?

_____

_____

_____

Takeaway Truth

God cares for all people. God has gifted you with a way to serve others; He has given you something that others need. God has also given you a platform, an audience, a circle of influence to serve within. In most cases you don't have to look very far to see the needs around you. Now go and live today searching for and serving those in need of all that God's given you to "pay forward"!

Valor Prayer

GIVING LORD, You have called me and gifted me to serve, not for acclaim, but to bless Your people and to build Your kingdom. Show me where I can serve You, and grant me the humility to give my life for others. Open my eyes to the needs of people around me, and give me wisdom to know how I can help meet them.

For Further Investigation

→ John 13:5-17
→ Mark 10:41-45
→ Galatians 5:13

Family
Engaged at Home

*"The measure of a man is the spiritual and emotional health of
his family. A real provider has a vision for a marriage that bonds
deeply, for sons with character as strong as trees, and for daughters
with confidence and deep inner beauty. Without that vision and
leadership, a family struggles, gropes, and may lose its way."*
—Stu Weber

Read & Reflect

Read and reflect on Job 1:1-5. Consider the following question:
What does a godly father look like?

_____

_____

_____

_____

The Challenge

Sometimes we see a godly father in an unlikely place. By common consensus Job was the "greatest of all the people of the east."
He was a wealthy landowner and extremely successful rancher.
He oversaw vast herds of camels, sheep, oxen, and donkeys. He
had an army of servants to attend to his wants and needs. He
was most highly regarded among his peers, and many sought his
advice on a variety of matters. When Job walked through the city,
young men bowed, old men stood in respect, even princes gave
way in his wake. He was a very busy and important man. Yet even
this rich, powerful, and famous man loved his children and knew

what was most important in their lives.

Job regularly prayed for his sons and daughters. He consistently offered sacrifices to consecrate them to the Lord. And he had a realistic understanding of his kids. He knew that his children could have sinned, so he kept them before God always.

And not only did Job pray for his family, he modeled godliness before them. He was "blameless and upright, one who feared God and turned away from evil." His children did not see one dad before the altar and a different dad in their house during the week. They never had to hear, "Do as I say, not as I do!" in their home. And God blessed Job with children who loved each other as well as their dad. He can do the same for us.

Living It Out

Some 30 years ago, Dr. James Dobson left a successful career at Children's Hospital in Southern California to help people "focus on the family." The Christian psychologist offered sound advice rooted in Scripture, and a growing number of people started responding with words of gratitude. He never imagined the impact he would have through more than 20 best-selling books and a radio broadcast heard around the globe.

In his book *Gadzooks* on the life and leadership principles of Dr. Dobson, Paul Batura described a man passionate about the family—God's family, his own family, his staff family, and families everywhere. "He rarely has a minute to spare in the course of a day but will take an hour to talk with a hurting, single mom or a lonely, elderly man," he wrote. "He is persistent when trying to find a fact but patient with his family and the foibles of his staff. He's a friend of the powerful but a defender of the weak."

Today he ministers through the Dr. James Dobson Family Institute. Though he has his share of detractors and takes a lot of heat in the media, Dr. Dobson is committed to pressing on in support of family related issues. "I will consider my earthly existence to have been wasted unless I can recall a loving family, a consistent investment in the lives of people, and an earnest attempt to serve the God who made me," maintains Dr. Dobson. "Nothing else makes much sense."

→ What kind of family did you grow up in?

_____

_____

_____

_____

→ If you're married and have a family, how does your family differ from the one you grew up in? How is it similar?

_____

_____

_____

_____

→ Why is it absolutely essential to remember that a man's primary discipleship responsibility is his family?

_____

_____

_____

_____

Takeaway Truth

God is our Father. He loves you and created you to love. Think about it, the God of the universe, who holds all of creation in His hand, created you to be in relationship with Him! If you're not a husband or father, commit now to carry out these future roles, as the Lord leads, for His glory. As a husband or father, your responsibility is to place your wife and children's hands in God's hand so they may know Him better and experience His love. Now go and live today as a child of God, loved and cherished by your Creator, and take spiritual responsibility in your home!

Valor Prayer

HEAVENLY FATHER, give me a vision to be a godly father. I pray that I can be a model for my family and my brothers and sisters. Help me to communicate Your love to my wife, to my kids and to my extended family in Christ. Watch over my family and keep them in Your care.

For Further Investigation

→ Ephesians 5:22-6:4

→ Psalm 127

→ 1 Timothy 5:8

The Church
Building Up Others

"The church of Christ is not supposed to be a group of harmless, irrelevant, mind-your-own-business worshipers who gather once a week, tucked away from anything public, just to practice their form of religion. . . .Nothing could be more unbiblical. The purpose behind this satanically inspired dogma is to keep the Church from being the Church—the ekklesia."
—Dutch Sheets

Read & Reflect

Read and reflect on Acts 2:42-47. Consider the following question: *What does authentic friendship among fellow Christians look like?*

_____

_____

_____

_____

The Challenge

The city of Jerusalem was in an uproar! The followers of Jesus of Nazareth, who had been crucified, claimed that He had risen from the dead. And they were preaching and healing the sick in His name, much to the chagrin of the Jewish leaders. Like any new religious movement, some in the city believed, some were antagonistic, and many were simply looking to see if there was any substance to the faith they were preaching. Were these new believers charlatans? Were they sincere but misguided dupes? Or was their faith real? Could they really be in touch with the living God?

One need only look at the way they related to each other to answer these questions. These people were *devoted*—not only to the teaching of their new religion, but also to one another. When they rubbed shoulders with each other, genuine love was the result. They not only worshiped together, they delighted in taking care of one another. If someone had a need, they tripped over each other trying to be the first to fill it.

Their faith overcame social and political boundaries of all kinds. Masters sang and took communion with slaves. Later, Jews would sit and eat with Gentiles. Those with more gave freely to those with less. They ate together in each other's homes, gladly and generously sharing what they had. Their common beliefs spilled out into authentic love for one another. "And the Lord added to their number day by day those who were being saved.." He can do the same today.

Living It Out

Gene Getz believes what the Bible says about Christians, "so we, though many, are one body in Christ, and individually members one of another" (Romans 12:5). That is, we are a family, and all of the "one another" and "each other" verses in the Bible have everything to do with a healthy, vibrant family—when practiced!

In the introduction to his book *Building Up One Another*, Gene says that the Lord brought this home to him as a Dallas Theological Seminary professor. His students would ask him such questions as, "What is a healthy church?", "What does God expect from all believers?", "What makes a church a dynamic witness in the world?"

As he searched the Scriptures for answers, Gene says, "Again and again I noticed exhortations regarding what believers are to do *for one another*." So in 1972, he put feet to what he saw as authentic Christian fellowship and started Fellowship Bible Church in Dallas. Since then he's helped to launch a number of branch Fellowship Bible Churches, and he presently pastors one in Plano, Texas. In addition, he heads the Center for Church Renewal and has a syndicated radio program, "Renewal," to do everything he can to help Christians truly become the family the Bible says we are and calls us to be.

→ What is a healthy church?

_____

_____

_____

_____

→ What does God expect from all believers?

_____

_____

_____

_____

→ What is it that makes a church a dynamic witness in the world?

_____

_____

_____

_____

Takeaway Truth

God has one body with many members. God created and designed His body of believers to be complete and sufficient to glorify Himself. You are part of the body of Christ, and the body is incomplete without you. Now that should give you something to think about! The question for you is, what are your gifts and how are you using them within the body of Christ? Now go and live today seeking and fulfilling the specific part you play in building up Christ's church!

Valor Prayer

FATHER GOD, thank You for my new family, my brothers and sisters in Christ. Help me to love them, to care for them, to give sacrificially for them. Help us as a church to love one another. Show me how You have gifted me to serve the body of Christ, and give me strength to be a servant.

For Further Investigation

→ Romans 1:11-12
→ Philippians 2:1-4
→ Romans 16:1-16

The World
Reaching the Lost

"If you're in a job with a bunch of bad people who curse and swear and tell coarse jokes, I don't feel a bit sorry for you. They're probably why you're there."
—Jerry Cook

Read & Reflect

Read and reflect on Matthew 9:9-13. Consider the following question: *What does authentic friendship with nonbelievers look like?*

The Challenge

When Jesus explained to His disciples why He had come, He simply said, "For the Son of Man came to seek and to save the lost." In order to accomplish His mission, Jesus not only preached the Gospel, but He chose twelve men to be with Him. He spent most of His three-year ministry hanging out with the twelve, living with them, eating with them, modeling life for them, and training them to carry out His mission after He was gone. But He did not live in a "holy huddle," completely separated from unbelievers. He was not afraid to touch the lives of the unclean, the outcasts, and the sinners.

Here Jesus went to the home of the tax gatherer, Matthew, also called Levi, whom He had just called to be one of His followers. Along with Matthew are many of his fellow tax gatherers and their friends, who are called "sinners." They were probably thugs, hired by the tax gatherers to help "collect" the taxes, along with prostitutes and other unsavory characters.

But there, comfortably in their midst, was Jesus, carrying out His mission. He knew that to save the lost, He had to spend some time with them, He had to show mercy to them, and He had to let His life rub off on them. He ate with them, talked with them, shared the Good News with them, all in the context of love for them. And they were drawn to Jesus by His love. God can do the same with us.

Living It Out

Before he met President George Bush, Sr., William Wallace Brown, Jr., was a homeless and bitter man. For 15 years he lived on the streets and stewed over the memory of how a lawyer had swindled him out of his home.

Then, in 1989, he caught sight of the president entering St. John's Episcopal Church, across from the White House. "Will you pray for me?" he asked.

"No," responded the president, startling both William and the church members who overheard him. Then, with a warm, inviting smile of friendship, the president said, "Come inside with us and pray for yourself."

William prayed for himself that day. And from then until his death on October 17, 2000, he attended the eight o'clock service at the "church of presidents" and never failed to pray for the powerful and powerless of the nation. Rev. Luis Leon said William was a man who "really understood that the kingdom of God is for all of us." And it all began when the president extended true friendship with an invitation to "come on in."

→ Is the group you hang with "all over the map" in terms of faith or a "holy huddle"?

_____

_____

_____

→ To what extent are you influenced by or influencing the world around you?

_____

_____

_____

→ If you're to have an even greater impact on nonbelievers where you live and work, what needs to change? What's your plan?

_____

_____

_____

Takeaway Truth

God loved the *world* so much that He sent His one and only Son, Jesus, that whoever believed in Him would spend eternity in His loving care (see John 3:16). Simply put, God loves everyone. He wants all people to receive His message of salvation through a relationship with His Son, Jesus Christ. God created and designed us to share His message with others. You have likes/dislikes, dreams, skills, and passions that He has placed within you so that you might have life—life to the full—and share in His plan for salvation. Now go and live today, fully alive, proclaiming your testimony as a man who has something significant to offer!

Valor Prayer

MERCIFUL LORD, You were the friend of sinners during Your time on earth. Empower me to love my neighbors, my co-workers, and all with whom I come into contact. Help me to see all people as You see them, with compassion and mercy. And give me courage to invite them to "come on in."

For Further Investigation

→ Matthew 5:14-16

→ Romans 12:9-21

→ 1 Peter 3:13-17

Purpose
Living with Intention

*"It is not what a man does that determines
whether his work is sacred or secular,
but why he does it."*
—A. W. Tozer

Read & Reflect

Read and reflect on 1 Corinthians 9:1-27. Consider the following
question: *How can a man live a purpose-driven life?*

_____

_____

_____

_____

The Challenge

As a Roman citizen, Paul had rights that few Jews had under the
rule of the emperor. And as an apostle of Christ, Paul could have
justly requested wages from his disciples. But rather than demand
his rights, Paul became a servant of all. He voluntarily limited his
own freedoms, gave up a lucrative career as a tentmaker and went
hungry, submitted to beatings and humiliation, even denied himself a loving wife. Why would a man do all this? He did it because
he had a purpose, a vision, a calling from God. Paul gave up everything temporal in life to accomplish his purpose of preaching
the Gospel and winning the lost to Christ. He was so gripped by
his vision that he was willing to "endure anything rather than put
an obstacle in the way of the gospel of Christ." How does a man

achieve this single-minded, purpose-driven life?

Paul used to be known as Saul of Tarsus, a highly educated Pharisee, expert in the Law of God, and a persecutor of Christians. When Jesus dramatically called Paul to follow Him, the Pharisee became an apostle of Christ, and his life was radically changed. Keenly aware of his own sin, Paul was awed by the grace and mercy of God. Deeply understanding his own unworthiness, Paul was overwhelmed by God's love for him. Acutely realizing how much he deserved God's wrath, Paul was filled with gratitude for God's forgiveness. Because Christ had given His life for Paul, the apostle freely gave his all for Christ.

One word summed up Paul's way of following Christ: *Discipline!* "So I do not run aimlessly; I do not box as one beating the air. But I discipline my body and keep it under control, lest after preaching to others I myself should be disqualified." By the power of the Holy Spirit, Paul exercised stern self-control, making each moment of his life subject to his purpose of making disciples of Christ. Paul gave up many activities he was free to do in order to win others to Christ: not legalistically, not trying to win favor with God, not trying to impress others. And God blessed him greatly. He does the same for us.

Living It Out

Who's the most on-purpose person you know of today? It's likely Rick Warren, author of the bestsellers *The Purpose Driven Church* and *The Purpose Driven Life*. His books have sold in the millions and continue to influence a countless number of people.

Imagine, it all began in Southern California's Orange County decades earlier, when young Pastor Rick told 60 people at the very first Saddleback trial service about a dream God had given him—a dream of a church 20,000-people strong, reaching out with Jesus' touch to the hurting, depressed, frustrated, and confused, and home base for sharing the Good News worldwide.

Today that's reality. What's more, God has expanded Rick's purpose. He says the next 25 years will be seeing his "P.E.A.C.E. Plan" become a reality. It's about *Planting* churches, *Equipping* servant leaders, *Assisting* the poor, *Caring* for the sick, and *Educating* the next generation (see www.thepeaceplan.com). The aim is "mobilizing a billion Christians to tackle the global giants of spiritual lostness, egocentric leadership, poverty, disease, and illiteracy." His life reflects how God can use one ordinary man who is impassioned by God's purpose to impact eternity.

⟶✦⟵

✦ It's said that if you aim at nothing, you're sure to hit it. How does that reflect your life?

_____

_____

_____

_____

✦ What would God have as the "bull's-eye" of your aim?

_____

_____

_____

_____

✦ What step(s) might you determine to make today to better live an on-purpose life?

_____

_____

_____

_____

Takeaway Truth

God has the perfect plan. God is holy, self-sufficient, and timeless. He does not need anything from us, yet He created us to be in relationship with Him so that we may glorify Him. Our purpose here on earth is to share His Gospel, the Good News of Jesus Christ, so that He will receive the Glory. You are uniquely created and loved by the Maker of the universe for this purpose. Now go and live today as a man fully alive in Jesus Christ, glorifying your Creator with your life by living out the plan He has for your life!

Valor Prayer

SOVEREIGN LORD, I want a purpose in life that will make a difference in people's lives for eternity. Show me the calling and vision You have for me, and empower me to discipline my life to accomplish it. Keep me from side tracks as I bow down to You and give You my whole life in order to bring glory to Your name.

For Further Investigation

→ Matthew 28:18-20

→ 1 Corinthians 15:1-11

→ Philippians 3:12-14

Legacy

Passing on a Godly Heritage

*"Our children will define the future, which makes them
our most significant and enduring legacy. After all, God
never told his followers to take over the world through
force or intelligence. He simply told us to have children
and then raise them to honor God in all they do."*
—George Barna

Read & Reflect

Read and reflect on Joshua 24:14-27. Consider the following
question: *What's the greatest gift a man can leave behind?*

_____

_____

_____

_____

The Challenge

Joshua, the leader of Israel, was getting old and tired. He, along
with Caleb, had spent 40 years wandering around Mount Sinai
through no fault of their own. Joshua had led the Israelites into
the Promised Land; he had fought their battles and organized
their territories, all under the Lordship of Yahweh, the God of
Abraham, Isaac, and Jacob. Now in his last years, he turned his
attention to his legacy. What would he leave behind? Were all the
years of toil and warfare worth it? With these questions in mind,
Joshua assembled the people for his last address to them. It was
clear to see his passion—the thing that he most wanted to leave

behind, what he longed to be written as his epitaph.

What burned in Joshua's heart was the desire to leave behind a people who served the Lord; his own family first, then the nation of Israel. "But as for me and my house, we will serve the Lord!" Joshua exclaimed. He then pushed the people to make a commitment, either serve God or idols. He forced them into a choice, and they chose the Lord.

Joshua's eyes were focused beyond this world. Huge bank accounts and vast properties are great gifts to anyone's children, but they are only temporary. Joshua wanted his children, and his people, to join him in eternity. He wanted God's name to be exalted, even after he was gone. And "Israel served the Lord all the days of Joshua, and all the days of the elders who outlived Joshua and had known all the work that the Lord did for Israel." God can grant the same legacy today.

Living It Out

Would baseball be his legacy? In some very small circles, yes, Billy Sunday left a legacy in his stint with the Chicago White-stockings starting in 1883. Well surpassing his baseball career, though, was his monumental ministry as an American evangelist whose fame peaked from 1914 to 1919.

Baseball had brought this youngest son of a Union soldier to Chicago. While his father died when Billy was only five weeks old, Billy met his heavenly Father in response to preaching at the Pacific Garden Mission. Before long his heart pulled away from baseball and toward lay evangelism work, and he began to help evangelist J. Wilbur Chapman with his revival meetings. When Chapman stepped aside, Billy started holding his own meetings.

Through the years invitations to speak as well as audience numbers grew. In the two-month period of May and June 1917, he preached 120 salvation-centered sermons in New York City. Upon his death in 1935, Billy left a legacy not of an institution but an estimated *one million people* who took him up on his invitation to walk "the sawdust trail" to come to the Father through His Son, Jesus.

→ Everyone leaves a legacy, for better or worse. What's the legacy you're working on today?

_____

_____

_____

_____

→ What would you like people to say about you at the end of your life? If this is a pipe dream in light of how you're living your life today, what needs to change?

_____

_____

_____

_____

→ As for you and your house, whom will you serve? Choose this day!

_____

_____

_____

_____

Takeaway Truth

God's legacy is eternal. As part of His legacy, we will worship Him in heaven for ever and ever, amen! The best legacy we can leave behind in our brief time here on earth is to honor our Creator and Savior by living out the Great Commission (Matthew 28:18-20) in light of the Greatest Commandment and Second Like It (Matthew 22:34-40), so that it may be said about us that we loved God with everything that's within us; that we loved our neighbors as ourselves; and that we followed Jesus' example of making disciples of all nations. Now go and live today, loving God and all that matters to Him, leaving a legacy *for the Gospel and generations!*

Valor Prayer

EVERLASTING FATHER, give me the heart of Joshua. You have placed only two eternal things on this earth: Your Word and people. Help me not to be sidetracked by the call of this world. Help me to give my life for these eternal things, beginning with my own family and spreading to everyone around me.

For Further Investigation

→ 2 Timothy 2:1-7
→ Exodus 34:1-7
→ Deuteronomy 6:4-9

Going Forward

Well done! You've finished a journey. . . . But really, this journey is just beginning. Here's how you can keep in the right race at the right pace.

First, it is imperative that you continue the journey by meeting with God every day. How do you make that practical? We recommend starting out with 10 minutes a day with what we call "Take 10" with God.

If someone tells you to "take 10," they're telling you to stop what you're doing and take a 10-minute break.

Sometimes that break can't come soon enough! We live in such a fast-paced world we can be in danger of wearing ourselves out if we don't press the pause button from time to time.

That goes for our spiritual lives as well. We know in our heart of hearts that we need to take a "time out" to be with God every day. We know the benefits of doing so . . . and we know what happens when we fail to do so—we're either revitalized or drained spiritually!

Here are just a few Bible verses that remind us why it's important to take time out with God:

➜ "Be still, and know that I am God; I will be exalted among the nations, I will be exalted in the earth." —Psalm 46:10

➜ "Come near to God and he will come near to you." —James 4:8a

➜ "Very early in the morning, while it was still dark, Jesus got up, left the house and went off to a solitary place, where he prayed." —Mark 1:35

There's an old saying, "You deserve a break today!" If we are to live in light of these and many other Bible verses, we need a "spiritual break" each day! And a good start is by thinking of it this way: **"Take 10" with God!**

So how might you spend those *ten precious minutes?* Many people have found it beneficial to focus on getting into the Bible and talking with God about what they read and about everyday life. With this in mind, you might consider starting this way:

3 minutes – *Read the Bible.* How can anyone keep on the right and best path, "on the path of purity? By living according to your word" (Psalm 119:9).

3 minutes – *Meditate on what you read.* Consider three questions: *What does it say? What does it mean? And what does it mean to me?* How can anyone stay on the best, most blessed path? "Blessed is the one . . . whose delight is in the law of the Lord, and who meditates on his law day and night" (Psalm 1:1-2).

4 minutes – *Pray.* A great way to pray is the "ACTS" Plan, giving a minute each to the following four topics: **A**doration, **C**onfession, **T**hanksgiving, **S**upplication. Jesus Himself said, "But when you pray, go into your room, close the door and pray to your Father, who is unseen. Then your Father, who sees what is done in secret, will reward you" (Matthew 6:6).

Here's the thing. You start with 10 minutes a day, and before long it becomes a habit! Not only that, before long you find you're able to stretch that 10 minutes into 15 . . . even a half hour or more! To be revitalized or drained spiritually—the choice is yours!

Here's how the psalm-writer David put it: "You, God, are my God, earnestly I seek you; I thirst for you, my whole being longs for you, in a dry and parched land where there is no water" (Psalm 63:1).

When's the best time for you to "Take 10" with God—in the morning, midday, or evening? Why not give it a try and see how the Lord leads? *You deserve a break today*—and you'll be glad you did!

Second, if you've processed this study Side-by-Side or in a triad or small group setting, remember that Warrior Brothers continue to "be there" for one another. Commit to pray for and encourage one another. Pick up resources you feel would help your Warrior Brothers continue the Mighty Men of Valor journey. Keep the lines of communication open so you can catch up on others' lives, give updates on the progress you've made on issues that surfaced during this study, and have an extended prayer time together.

Finally, look around and consider if there's a person or another group of men with whom you would like to process this material. As Solomon said, "Two are better than one" (Ecclesiastes 4:9); and as the writer of Hebrews added, "And let us consider how to stir up one another to love and good works, not neglecting to meet together" (Hebrews 10:24-25a). Never go it alone. Always have a Warrior Brother at your side, and always be there for the men in your sphere of influence.

The Lord is with you, Mighty Man of Valor! May He continue to bless and lead you.

About the Authors

Dean Ridings, Bob Jones, and Scott Ballenger are founding members of Make a Mark Ministries—see www.makeamark.net. They are actively involved in a variety of disciple-making and men's ministry initiatives.

Dean is a pastor and director of biblical counseling and discipleship at Calvary Worship Center in Colorado Springs. He has an MA, an M.Div. and a Th. D. Dean also serves as affiliate faculty at Colorado Christian University. Dean and Kim have four married children. Email him at dean@makeamark.net.

Bob has a Th. M. and teaches theology part-time at Grand Canyon University. He and his wife, Kate, have three grown children and five grandchildren. Bob and Kate live in Peoria, Arizona. You can contact Bob at bob@makeamark.net.

Scott has a Bachelor of Science in Computer Science and is a senior engineer at VMware. The father of two adult children, Scott and his wife, Robin, live in Colorado Springs. Email Scott at scott@makeamark.net.

For information about Make a Mark Ministries, our ministry initiatives, and other resources we have developed "for the gospel and generations," find us online at www.makeamark.net.

A Make a Mark Ministrics Bible Study Series
www.makeamark.net

Mighty Men of Valor have three distinct characteristics: Strength, Courage & Passion

Men need Strength that comes from God alone, the kind of strength He gave men like Gideon—who lived at a time when everyone did what was right in their own eyes—David and his band of mighty men, and Jesus' early church followers!

Men need Courage to stand strong in increasingly challenging times, because we live in a world that's not what God created—evil exists, and as someone has said, "All it takes for evil to flourish is good men to stand by and do nothing"!

Men need Passion to live in light of the fact that the God of the universe chose us to be His children, called us to be kingdom men, and enables us to passionately live like Jesus and advance His Gospel where we live, work, and play through the generations!

Go through the entire Mighty Men of Valor series!

1. Use these studies as a daily devotional. We strongly encourage every man to take time out for a daily meeting—or appointment—with God.
2. Work through these studies with another man. Think of this as walking "Side-by-Side," meeting weekly for mutual growth, support, and accountability.
3. Connect with other men in a triad or small-group setting. Think of Jesus, who invested in a small group of 12 men, guiding them on the spiritual journey.

To order titles in the Mighty Men of Valor series:
www.makeamark.net

ARE YOU LIVING WITH KINGDOM-MINDED PURPOSE?

This is God's desire for you . . . The journey awaits!

"And this gospel of the kingdom will be proclaimed throughout the whole world as a testimony to all nations, and then the end will come." —**Jesus** (Matthew 24:14)

"If we have a limited time with someone, we would want him or her to fully grasp the **gospel of the Kingdom** and its implications."

That's the heart behind this workbook. We would want men and women to take what we call the **Kingdom Life journey**, passing the following signposts along the way:

✔ Seeing the Kingdom Vision

✔ Relating to the King

✔ Representing the King

✔ Living with Kingdom-Minded Purpose

Ideal for one-to-one and small-group processing, each of the 12 lessons will help you SEE, SEARCH, STAND, and SHOW life-changing Kingdom principles.

Join the journey and see the gospel of the Kingdom advance deeper in your own heart and make an eternal difference in the lives of those around you!

Make a Mark
MINISTRIES

FIND "THE KINGDOM LIFE JOURNEY" ON AMAZON OR
WWW.MAKEAMARK.NET

Tap into this free series to help "Ignite the Kingdom Life" within you!

Asked if he was the long-anticipated Messiah, John the Baptist pushed back immediately—that's Jesus! Yet he did take the opportunity to speak of God's mission for his life:

> *"I'm baptizing you here in the river, turning your old life in for a kingdom life. The real action comes next: The main character in this drama—compared to him I'm a mere stagehand—will **ignite the kingdom life** within you, a fire within you, the Holy Spirit within you, changing you from the inside out"* (Matthew 3:11 MSG).

We have developed a series of one-page monographs to help **Ignite the Kingdom Life**—all freely available as PDF downloads and may be reproduced for ministry! They'll help you:

✔ Get to Know God

✔ Get into God's Word

✔ Talk to God . . . Pray

✔ Walk With Jesus Day by Day

✔ Live in Light of the Spiritual Battle

Print them out, process and pray through them, keep a few in your Bible to pass along to fellow Christians who long to make a Kingdom difference in everyday life!

Download the entire set free of charge at:
www.makeamark.net

Made in the USA
Coppell, TX
05 June 2021

56910536R00037